D1309441

DRUGS AND AIDS

Teens are one of the fastest-growing groups who are at risk of getting HIV.

DRUGS AND AIDS

Barbara Hermie Draimin, DSW

THE ROSEN PUBLISHING GROUP, INC.

NEW YORK

The people pictured in this book are only models; they in no way, practice or endorse the activities illustrated. Captions serve only to explain the subjects of the photographs and do not imply a connection between the real-life models and the staged situations shown. News agency photographs are exceptions.

Published in 1994 by The Rosen Publishing Group, Inc.
29 East 21st Street, New York, NY 10010

First Edition

Library of Congress Cataloging-in-Publication Data
Draimin, Barbara Hermie.
    Drugs and aids / Barbara Hermie Draimin.
      — 1st ed.
      p.   cm. — (The Drug abuse prevention library)
    Includes bibliographical references and index.
    ISBN 0-8239-1702-9
    1. AIDS (disease) in adolescence—Juvenile
      literature.   2. Intravenous drug abuse—Juvenile
      literature. [1. AIDS (disease)   2. Drug abuse.]
        I. Title   II. Series.
    RJ387.A25D73   1994   94-2331
      616.97′92—dc20   CIP
                                                          AC

Manufactured in the United States of America

Contents

Chapter 1 Sarah and David *7*

Chapter 2 HIV and AIDS *12*

Chapter 3 Getting AIDS from Drug Use *19*

Chapter 4 Getting AIDS from Having Sex *25*

Chapter 5 Preventing AIDS *34*

Chapter 6 Drug Treatment *43*

Chapter 7 What You Can Do *55*

Help List *59*

Glossary—Explaining New Words *61*

For Further Reading *62*

Index *63*

It helps to have a close friend to talk to about your thoughts and fears.

CHAPTER 1

Sarah and David

Sarah and David met in a hospital waiting room. Both of them had appointments with Dr. Brooks, who was late. Sarah and David had seen each other before in the waiting room, and now they struck up a conversation. They both knew that Dr. Brooks was an expert in teens and HIV. Each wondered if the other were infected.

Sarah spoke first. "I go to Jefferson High; how about you?"

David replied nervously, "I go to Walton." He paused a moment, then asked, "What do you think of Dr. Brooks?"

8 Sarah was glad of the question. Doctors and illness were what she really wanted to talk about, but she was scared.

"I like the doctor a lot. She always has time to listen to me. And I feel that what I say to her is private. She's not pushing me to do something or be different. She treats me like an adult. She gives me choices. What do you think?"

David said that he liked the doctor, but he felt bad about not getting better. He always seemed to have some germ. As soon as he got over one thing, some other rash broke out.

Dr. Brooks came rushing in. "I'm so sorry you had to wait so long. I had an emergency."

Sarah and David began to see each other often in the waiting room and talk. One day David waited until Sarah had seen the doctor and asked her if she wanted to go for pizza.

At Joe's Pizza, they talked endlessly about HIV and AIDS. Sarah and David had never before shared their secrets with anyone except family.

Sarah

Sarah had run away from home at 16 and begun using crack cocaine. At first

The injecting drug user often begins the use of drugs with a gateway drug such as alcohol or marijuana.

she got the drugs free from one of the people she hung out with. Then she was hooked and needed money to keep on buying. Soon she was having sex for money every day. She was known as a "working girl." She began getting infections and finally went to the doctor. Tests for sexual diseases showed that she had syphilis and HIV.

David

David was popular. He was on the football team, and he got good grades. When he was 15 he had sex with a girl in his

9

10 class. They dated for a while, but she began seeing one of his buddies. When he was 16 he had sex with a few more girls. The guys he hung out with were always talking about girls and sex. He thought that a lot of them were making it up.

One night a friend asked him if he wanted to hang out with a bunch of guys. David said okay and ended up at a club with bisexual men. He enjoyed the evening. The guys were friendly, and nobody boasted about conquering girls.

After a few nights at the club, David went home with one of the guys and had sex. The next day he felt confused and scared. He promised himself he would never go back to that club.

David began to drink a lot. When he closed his eyes to go to sleep, he kept seeing the guys in the club. But he was determined not to go back there.

He began dating girls again. They would go out to dinner, and if he had enough drinks, they would have sex. Later he would drop by the men's club for a nightcap. He didn't want to go, but he couldn't stop.

One night after drinking, David was in a serious car accident. The doctors said that he had to enter a detox program and learn to live without alcohol. He was also tested for HIV, and the result was positive. David felt as if his life was over.

Sarah and David had heard about HIV at school and on television. But neither one believed that they could get it. HIV was for adults who were drug addicts or gay. Sarah never took drugs with a needle. David thought he was safe since he wasn't gay.

David and Sarah both met with counselors once a week and attended support groups. David went to Alcoholics Anonymous meetings every day to make sure that he didn't drink any more. Since the accident, he was not allowed to drive. He stayed close to home and spent time taking care of his health.

David and Sarah called themselves the odd couple. They could hang out together without having to pretend or make up stories. They spent hours and hours talking about getting AIDS. Who would get sick first? Would they die? Would a cure be found before they got real sick? How long did people with HIV live?

HIV and AIDS

*H*IV is the virus that experts believe causes AIDS. Its full name is human immunodeficiency virus. It can get into the body four ways:

1. By dirty needles used to inject drugs such as heroin or steroids
2. By unprotected sexual intercourse
3. By being passed from mother to newborn baby
4. By blood transfusion before 1985.

The virus cannot get into the body from insect bites, toilet seats, saliva, hugging and kissing, or sneezes. Once HIV is in the body, it can multiply quietly for 10 years or more while the person can look

Anyone can get AIDS.

14 totally healthy. There is no way to know that a person has HIV unless he or she has been tested and tells you.

Testing

The test for HIV is done on a little blood from a vein in the arm. Examination shows whether the blood contains anti-bodies that fight the virus. The test is given at hospitals, clinics, and HIV test sites. It is often free, and in some places you don't have to give your name. Some states and provinces will test teens only if a parent is with them. In any case it is good to take along a trusted adult or friend to give you support and to remember things you might forget. Results of an HIV test usually take two weeks. For more information on testing, see the "Help List" on page 59.

AIDS

Sooner or later, people with HIV get sick. They get weak and cannot fight off germs, and the illness grows into AIDS, acquired immunodeficiency syndrome.

AIDS was discovered in 1981. Since it is a new disease, there are many rumors and false beliefs about it. Some people think that teenagers can't get AIDS. *They*

People with HIV need support and kindness.

16 *are wrong!* Anyone can get AIDS. But there are ways to make sure that you never get HIV.

No one knows where HIV came from or where it first started. Almost every country has AIDS. Africa and the United States have the most cases.

Having AIDS means that the HIV is no longer resting in the body. It is killing the good cells that fight disease. So people with AIDS have many different illnesses. They often get pneumonia and rashes that are hard to cure.

How Is AIDS Different from Other Diseases?

Several things make AIDS different from diseases like cancer or heart disease.

1. Because it is new, there is much for everyone to learn. Doctors and parents and children and teachers are all learning about AIDS at the same time.
2. HIV is acquired by having unprotected sex and by injecting drugs. No other disease is just like it.
3. Anyone can get HIV; however, homosexuals and injecting drug users have been hit the hardest,

and they are sometimes blamed for the disease by prejudiced people. People who contract cancer are not blamed. People who have heart attacks are not blamed. Blame and prejudice are other things that make AIDS different.

At present, no cure for AIDS is known. Doctors and researchers are working to find vaccines and cures.

When people find out that they have HIV, they know that their future will be hard. They need others to be kind and listen. We need to care for people with AIDS by giving them a smile or hug or helping with a task they need done.

Never make fun of a person with AIDS. Learn about AIDS and help keep the facts straight.

Talking about AIDS means talking about sex and drugs. Many people are afraid to talk about sex and drugs. A lot of people want to tell other people what to do. This book is about *you* deciding what *you* should do.

Remember:
- You can't get HIV from hugging.
- You can't get HIV from a swimming pool or toilet.

You can't tell if someone has HIV unless he or she tells you.

- You can't get HIV from a mosquito bite.
- You can't tell if someone has HIV unless he or she has been tested and tells you.

- You can get HIV as a teen.
- You can have HIV and look healthy.
- You can have HIV and not know it.

- You can prevent ever getting HIV.
- People with HIV need your support and kindness.

CHAPTER 3

Getting AIDS from Drug Use

*I*n this book drug use is defined as any substance taken into the body to change the mood or feeling without the direction of a doctor. Drugs can be alcohol such as beer or wine. They can be sleeping pills such as Seconal. They can be illegal drugs such as crack, cocaine, or marijuana. They can be drugs that are injected into a vein such as steroids or heroin. There are many slang names for drug users. Some crack smokers are called "beamers" or "thirst monsters" or "crackerjacks." Often, a part of using drugs is having a secret language.

Certain signs can give you a hint that a person you know may be taking drugs:

Certain signs can make you suspect that a person may be using drugs.

- Having track or needle marks on the arms or legs.
- Wearing sunglasses to hide red eyes.
- Wearing long sleeves to hide marks.
- Staying long in the bathroom (taking drugs in secret).
- Being late to school or work.
- Using breath mints to hide alcohol odor.
- Having big mood swings.
- Wearing messy and dirty clothing.
- Forgetting what was just said.
- Nodding off and falling asleep.
- Sweating even on cold days.
- Borrowing or begging for money.
- Being pushy, uptight, or nervous.
- Constantly sniffling and sneezing.
- Lying about everything.
- Never having any money.
- Hanging out with drug users.

Drug use can cause AIDS in two ways.

The first way is through injecting drugs with a dirty needle. This means putting a drug into a used hypodermic needle and putting the needle into a vein in the body. Heroin and steroids are two drugs that people shoot into their veins.

Don't let drugs do your thinking for you.

If a person uses a needle without cleaning it properly, blood containing HIV can be left in the needle and get into the user's blood. Many addicted drug users who want to protect themselves from HIV clean their needles with bleach and water.

You cannot get HIV when you give blood or when you get an injection from the doctor. The needles are used only once and then discarded.

The second way to get HIV from drugs is by letting drugs make decisions for you. When people use drugs, they often get silly, or tired, or high. They often forget to take care of themselves or others. For example, people who drink and drive go too fast and cause accidents. People who smoke marijuana and have sex sometimes don't use birth control. People who inject drugs may not bother to clean the needle or may have sex without using a condom.

Drugs often change the way people behave. Drugs make it harder to do the right thing. Drugs make people relax so much that they put themselves in great danger without realizing the risk. People on drugs pay attention only to getting more drugs. You may have heard stories about people taking LSD (acid) and jumping out of windows. But you rarely hear of people drinking and having unsafe sex. That's because so many people do it. But having unsafe sex can be just as dangerous as jumping out a window if your partner is HIV-positive.

Drugs and alcohol can cloud your judgement.

CHAPTER 4

Getting AIDS from Having Sex

*T*eenagers and female partners of injecting drug users are the fastest-growing
groups who are at risk of getting HIV.
They are being infected mostly by having
unprotected sex. The only way one can
be absolutely sure of not getting HIV
through sex is to have no sex.

What turns people on? Is it something
in the body that changes? Why are some
people heterosexual, some homosexual,
and some bisexual?

There are no clear answers to those
questions. Some experts think that people
choose their sexual orientation; other
experts think that people are born with
their orientation.

26 | *Heterosexual Sex*

As you know, heterosexual sex involves a man and a woman. Some people try out all kinds of sex. Some people wait to have sex until they find the one special person they want to be with for life. It is all right for teens and adults to want different things.

Many people consider themselves heterosexual because usually they prefer sex with someone of the other gender. But once in a while, they may have a homosexual experience.

The first important thing is to have sex only when *you* are ready. The second important thing is to have only protected sex.

Homosexual Sex

Homosexual sex means having sex with someone of the same gender. A boy has sex with another boy, or a girl has sex with a girl.

People who have sex with people of the same gender call themselves gay. Girls who are gay often use the term lesbian. Gays have realized that their favorite and often only kind of physical love is with a person of the same gender. When a gay man hears a romantic song, he thinks of a

Because of prejudice and stigma, it can be frightening
for people to admit that they might be gay.

28 man. When a lesbian sees a play about lovers, she thinks of a woman. Because of prejudice and stigma, it is scary for people to find out that they might be gay. Most homosexuals don't figure it out until they are in their twenties or thirties or even older. The discrimination against gays makes them do everything they can to avoid it.

There is a great difference between experimenting with same-gender sex and coming to the conclusion that you are homosexual.

That is important because many people think that only gays can get HIV. That is wrong for two reasons:

1. HIV is transferred through both homosexual and heterosexual sex.
2. Having unprotected sex is what passes the virus from person to person.

Bisexual Sex

People who are bisexual may have sex with people of the same gender or with people of the other gender. Many of them do not call themselves bisexual. They consider themselves either heterosexual or homosexual but sometimes have sex with the other group.

The important thing to remember is that any kind of sex can be risky.

How HIV Is Passed During Sex

Like all viruses, HIV cannot multiply outside the body. HIV is carried in body fluids during sex. Semen is the body fluid that comes out of a man's penis during sex. Sperm is carried in semen, and if HIV is present in the body, it can also be carried in semen.

The body fluid in a woman's vagina is called vaginal fluid. If HIV is present in the body, it can be carried in vaginal fluid.

HIV can also be carried in blood and transferred from an open sore or cut or from menstrual blood.

If HIV-infected blood or semen or vaginal fluid were to touch your hand, you would not get HIV. But if your hand had a deep bloody cut, the HIV could pass from the other person's body to yours.

"Sexual transmission" means that HIV passes from fluid to fluid (semen, vaginal fluid, blood) during sexual activity.

Three kinds of sexual activity make it

There are no clear answers as to why some people are heterosexual and others are homosexual.

easy to contract HIV: vaginal intercourse, oral intercourse, and anal intercourse.

Vaginal Intercourse

When a man puts his penis into a woman's vagina, HIV can pass from his semen into the woman's vaginal fluid. It can also go the other way, from vaginal fluid into the penis via the semen. A woman is ten times more likely to get HIV from a man than a man is from a woman.

If a woman with HIV becomes pregnant, she can give the virus to her baby while it is in the womb or during birth. One out of three babies of HIV-positive women gets the virus and develops AIDS.

Oral Intercourse

In this sexual activity, the mouth of a man or woman touches the sexual organs of a partner. Fluids from the sexual organs mix with fluids from the mouth. HIV passes more easily if there is a sore or cut in the mouth or on the sexual organs.

Anal Intercourse

When a man inserts his penis into the rectum (also called anus) of a man or woman, it is called sodomy. It is against

The only sex that is one hundred percent safe is no sex.

the law in a number of states. If there are sores in the anus, the HIV travels more easily from one body to the other.

Remember three important things about HIV and sex:

- One can choose *not* to have sex and have no risk of getting HIV sexually.
- Drugs like alcohol, marijuana, and cocaine are risky to use while having sex because they lower willpower and make people forget to be careful.
- One can choose to have sex and use protection. This is discussed in detail in the next chapter.

CHAPTER 5

Preventing AIDS

You can protect yourself from AIDS by not using drugs or having sex. Some people make fun of people who take care of themselves. They call those who say no "goody two-shoes." It may hurt to be called names by your peers, but "goody" can also mean kind, healthy, safe, and solid. If you think well of yourself, if you have high self-esteem, it is easy to stand up to name-calling.

Carey
Carey is sixteen and has a steady boyfriend, Kevin. Kevin has been asking her to have sex for the last six months, but Carey doesn't

want to until she is ready. She is afraid of pregnancy or even getting HIV. She wants to keep up her grade point average in hopes of winning a college scholarship.

Without help, she could not go to college at all. Her mother had three children before she was twenty years old and could barely feed and clothe them.

Carey loves her mother deeply and admires how hard she works. But she does not want the same life for herself. Ann, her 17-year-old sister, is pregnant and no longer attending school.

Carey is crazy about Kevin, but she does not want to have sex and does not like always talking about it. Kevin says that if Carey did get pregnant, he would be a good father and take care of them both. Carey does not want to be taken care of. She wants to be able to take care of herself. She also wants a boyfriend who takes care of himself.

Kevin is afraid that Carey will go off to college and meet someone else. While she is studying, he hangs out with the guys and drinks beer. His grades are going down while hers are going up. Carey wonders if Kevin is going to find another girlfriend since she won't give in. She wonders if she is strong enough to stand up for herself and maybe end up alone.

36 | ***"Don't Worry!"***
When a boyfriend or girlfriend tells you
not to worry, watch out. Usually it means
that he or she isn't worried. A boy does
not have to worry the way a girl does. He
is not the one who will become pregnant.
He is not the one who will carry the baby
in his body for nine months.

When a girl tells you not to worry
about having a few beers and driving
home, watch out. She isn't the one who
borrowed the car. She isn't the one who
can lose a driver's license. She isn't the
one who will feel responsible if someone
gets hurt in an accident.

It is smart to worry about yourself.
Many teens get into trouble with drugs,
sex, cars, and violence. One mistake can
change your whole life. It did for Sarah
and David in Chapter 1. There is an old
saying: "Better safe than sorry." Worrying
about yourself is a way to protect yourself
from danger. When you are scared, pay
attention to the message you are giving
yourself. You are the one who will live
with the results.

Having Sex and Preventing AIDS
It has been shown that people who have
sexually transmitted diseases (STDs) are

In order to have safer sex, the boy must wear a condom.

38 | more likely to get HIV also. If you get a disease such as gonorrhea, syphilis, chlamydia, or herpes, it is important to go to the doctor and take the medications you are given. Don't wait and hope that the disease will go away. It will just get worse and put you at greater risk for HIV. If you or your partner have any sores near or on your sexual organs, don't have sex until they are cured.

Some teens believe that the best way for both partners to be safe is to be tested and then be faithful. Deciding whether to be tested is difficult. Discuss it with an adult counselor first.

Suppose both of you are tested and both of you are negative. You must now decide whether you are 100 percent sure that neither you nor your partner will ever have unsafe sex with someone else or inject drugs.

The trouble with that is that you are betting your life on someone else's behavior. If your partner secretly has an unsafe affair, you become at risk for HIV and other diseases.

The safer way to protect yourself from HIV is for the boy to use a condom. Condoms for girls are now becoming available.

How to Use a Condom

- Check the date on the condom to make sure it is not old or dried out.
- Use a condom *every* time you have sex.
- Use condoms made of latex rubber.
- Use condoms made with the spermicide nonoxynol-9.
- Put the condom on when the penis is erect.
- Leave a small space at the tip of the condom to catch the semen.
- After climax, withdraw the penis while it is still erect.
- Throw out the condom, since it can be used only once.

If Your Partner Says No to Condoms

Your partner might say, "If you cared about me and trusted me you wouldn't want me to wear a condom. Maybe we shouldn't be together at all." Here are some things you can do if your partner doesn't want to wear a condom:

- Be open and discuss your fears and desires. If you can't agree on sex or protection, recognize that you both have a big problem.

40

- Don't make trouble for yourself by drinking or using drugs. You are putting yourself in a hot spot.
- Don't let someone else tell you what is best. If you're not sure, give yourself a few days to think about it. If you hear remarks such as "I'll leave you," or "Maybe you don't love me," run in the other direction. Real love means being patient. A caring lover does not make threats.

Having Sex and Using Drugs

There is a saying, "Willpower lasts two weeks and dissolves in alcohol." That means it is easy to make a promise but harder to keep it. Everybody has trouble with willpower. The only kind of willpower that works is the kind that you start every day with. If you start every day with a desire to diet, then each day it is possible to diet. Even if your willpower lasts long enough to take off the pounds, however, going back to the way you used to eat will put them back on.

It is hard to change things you do. If you want to stop smoking or start using condoms, it is hard to make the change.

And using drugs makes it almost impossible. Drugs lower your willpower.

Teens have two choices: be safe or take a risk with their health. Which will you choose?

Drugs such as alcohol or marijuana or cocaine make you feel mellow. They silence the voice in your mind that tells you what is best.

There are two voices in your mind. One says, "Be careful, do the right thing." The other one says, "Take a chance, do what you really want." These two voices argue frequently about whether to take chances. When you take drugs, you turn off the first voice and turn up the volume on the second voice. Drugs take away fears—even the ones you should have. If you take drugs before having sex, chances

42 are that it will be harder to be careful. People who drink often forget to use condoms, or else they decide that it doesn't really matter anyway.

In Chapter 1, David used alcohol to bury his pain and anger about liking men. He also drank to help him sleep with women when he didn't really want to. By drinking and not using condoms, he put himself, the men, and the women all at risk for HIV.

If You Can't Stop Using Drugs

Almost everyone who tries to stop using drugs has a few setbacks. That is okay as long as you don't give up. People who can't stop injecting drugs need to wear a condom every time they have sex and clean their needle every time they inject drugs.

The best plan for an injecting drug user is to get treatment. Drugs take control over people's lives. If you want to run your own life, you can't be hooked on drugs. Drugs take over as the leader of your life. People addicted to drugs will do anything to get drugs.

CHAPTER 6

Drug Treatment

*T*here are two steps to take in solving a drug problem: First, admit that you have a problem, and second, find the kind of help that works for you.

It is easy to tell if someone else is becoming addicted to drugs. It is very hard to know it is happening to yourself. You can't tell by the quantity. Some alcoholics need only one or two drinks to get drunk. Some people have one or two drinks before dinner every night and never become alcoholic. Some people can take drugs once in a while for fun. Others seem to get hooked on the high right away and want more and more.

44 Addicts need drugs in two ways. The first way is to calm the body physically. Once the body gets used to a drug, it wants more and more. Just as a cigarette smoker feels a need to light up, drinkers begin shaking if they don't have a drink. The body physically needs the drug.

The other way an addict needs a drug is to keep on feeling okay. Without the drug, the person may be very jittery or angry or sad or depressed.

Doctors use drugs to heal the body; they know how much of a drug to give and when. Addicts use drugs to stop the pain, but they don't know what drug to use or how much or when.

Sheila

Sheila was a good student and at thirteen was a year ahead in school. She studied at the library until just before dark. She hated to go home. Her mother and father fought nonstop every day. If Sheila or her brother Mack tried to stop it, the fight got even worse. Her parents argued over money, food, work, the apartment, her parents, his parents, and Sheila and Mack.

Sheila had two feelings at the same time. She wanted them to stay together, but she wanted them to break up if they couldn't stop

Using drugs doesn't make problems go away.

arguing. Her head was filled with their arguments. One day Mack and Sheila went for a walk, and he gave her some marijuana. "Try this," he said, "it will turn down the volume on Mom and Dad." Sheila was in such pain that she would have tried almost anything to get help.

At first Sheila liked the marijuana. She smoked a little as they walked and felt much more mellow when they got home. She even thought it helped her study because it took her mind off her parents.

But after two months Sheila was worse off than ever. The marijuana wasn't working any longer. She needed something stronger.

45

46   This is one of the ways that people become addicted. They start out being unable to solve a problem. They take a drug to ease the pain. After a while the drug no longer does the job and they need more or a different drug.

How else could Sheila and Mack have tried to deal with their problem? They needed to get help. One or both of them needed to go to a teacher or a counselor or a minister or a nurse and ask for help. They could not solve the problem within the family. An outsider was needed to help everyone in the family sort out their feelings. The parents had no idea how much pain they were causing Sheila and Mack. They thought they were doing the children a favor by staying together. Most families like to keep their problems within the family. But sometimes families can create problems that they can't solve without help.

Getting Help with a Drug Problem

It is possible to solve your drug problem, but it will take a lot of courage.

Sheila and Mack knew their first problem—hearing their parents fight. But sometimes people taking drugs

can't name their first problem. They just
know that they feel bad most of the
time.

*Tony's parents never fought, but they always
seemed to be apart. Dad worked late every
night, and Mom spent a lot of time next
door. They almost never had dinner as a
family. On holidays, it was very tense.
Everyone tried to be nice, but there were bad
vibes in every room. Tony thought that
maybe he was doing something wrong. He
went to see a counselor at school. The
counselor helped Tony figure out the problem.*

Admitting that you have a problem is
very tough. Many times people take the
drugs to cover up bad problems. If people
admit they have a drug problem and try
to get help, the next step is to deal with
the problem that was so painful in the
first place.

Using drugs creates an endless cycle:
Problem . . . pain . . . cover up with drugs
. . . addiction . . . more pain.

To break the cycle, one needs to give
up the drugs and then find out what
problems were causing the pain in the
first place.

To take on this big and important task,

Admitting that you have a drug problem can be difficult.

one needs *help*. It is almost always too hard to do alone.

There are many kinds of drug treatment. Some questions may help in choosing the right one for you or a friend:

- Which drugs are being used?
- Does the treatment take place away from home?
- Do you get help from one person, or is it a group treatment?
- How long does the treatment last?
- How much does it cost and who will pay?

Counseling

A counselor is someone whom you can talk to about your problems. Drug counselors often have had a drug problem themselves. You can find a drug counselor by calling one of the free numbers in the Help List on page 59.

There are two steps in treating drug problems. The first is to get the drugs out of your system. Depending on what drug you have been taking, that may require going to a hospital. Some drugs are so strong that it is important to be under the care of a doctor when you stop.

The next step is to handle the problem

50 that made you start taking drugs. If you don't cope with the problem, it will be very tempting to take drugs again and get back into the cycle.

Individual Help

Some people are very private. They don't want anyone to know that they have problems or what kind. Those people are usually more at ease with a solo or individual counselor.

Counselors listen to your problems. They cannot make feelings of loneliness or sadness go away. But they can help you admit to yourself that you feel bad and learn how to deal with it. They are caring people who will help you learn how to help yourself.

Couldn't you just talk to a friend? The problem is that the friend often has his or her own problems and may not have the time or patience to help with yours. Sometimes a friend gives specific advice that turns out badly. Counselors rarely give exact advice. They help you to figure out what you think is best to do.

If you know that you have a drug problem, it is time to seek outside help. If you are thinking about suicide, or someone else is very worried about you, seek

Friends are a great source of support.

help immediately. Talk to a trusted adult
right away. Or call a suicide hotline without delay. You can find one in the phone
directory under Samaritans or Suicide
Hotline.

Feelings can be scary and overwhelm-
ing. It is possible to have many different
feelings at the same time. And sometimes
it is hard to figure out where they all
came from.

People often fear that letting feelings
out is like opening Pandora's Box. They
are afraid that the feelings will overflow
and that they will never be able to get
control of themselves. That is rarely the

52 case. Usually searching out one's feelings is a relief. Pent-up feelings are the ones that cause harm.

How to Choose a Counselor

Just as each teacher at school is different, so is each counselor. You have probably been treated by doctors or nurses whom you liked a lot and some whom you liked less. One kind of person may make you feel jittery. Around another kind of person you may feel calm and sure of yourself. Part of that has to do with vibes. Sometimes we connect with people, and sometimes we don't.

Trust your own feelings about a counselor. If you take an instant dislike, go two or three times and see if you change your mind. If you still don't like the person, ask for another counselor.

It is okay to talk about any thoughts or feelings with the counselor. Counselors are trained to listen to anger, sadness, happiness, fear, or any other emotion you may have. This is not a place to be on "good behavior." It is a place to learn more about who you are and what makes you tick. You do not have to worry about the feelings of the counselor.

Other Sources of Help

Some teenagers can't talk when they are alone with an adult. They feel too strange. What if you can't get started?

Some counselors are teens. They have taken lessons in being peer counselors.

Some teenagers find it helpful to join a group of people who are all talking about their problems. Some groups have a counselor as leader. Other groups have no expert; these are called self-help groups. Self-help groups are usually free. You must promise you will never talk about anything said in the group. These groups teach members 12 steps to stop their addiction. Among the groups are Alcoholics Anonymous (AA) for drinkers and Narcotics Anonymous (NA) for people who use cocaine and heroin.

In these kinds of groups, you can hear people talk about problems like yours. It helps to know that you are not the only one in trouble.

You can go to a group and just listen. They will never force you to talk. But if you like the group and stay in it, you will probably want to share your ideas too.

Take care of yourself by being open and honest with your
boyfriend or girlfriend.

CHAPTER 7

What You Can Do

*T*here have been many ups and downs with AIDS. When the disease was first discovered, there was panic. When people kept dying and no one knew why, there was great fear. When the drug AZT was invented, there was great hope. Now it is known that AZT has only a little value. Doctors now say they don't know how long it will take to find a vaccine.

There are two things to keep in mind during the ups and downs. The first one is hope. We all hope and pray that HIV and AIDS will be conquered one day. The second is self-respect, being proud and wanting to take care of ourselves.

Help educate others about AIDS and HIV by sharing your knowledge.

You are an important part of the future. Preventing AIDS is the only sure way to solve the problem.
Here are things you can do:

1. Educate others.
2. Care about people with AIDS.
3. Fight racism, homophobia, and shame.
4. Protect yourself.

Educate Others
You now know a lot about HIV and
AIDS. When you hear other people pass-

ing rumors about HIV, speak up. So many false things are said about HIV. Spread the facts, not the disease.

Care about People with AIDS

People with AIDS are people like Sarah and David—nice people who made a big mistake. They need kindness and care. You cannot get AIDS by hugging them or holding their hands. You can run errands for them. You can treat them respectfully. Remember that no one wanted to get AIDS. Many people got AIDS before 1985 when no one knew how to guard against it. Never blame anyone for having HIV. He or she needs your love and support, not your criticism.

Fight Racism, Homophobia, and Shame

Each person deserves our help. Never be mean to people because of their race or homosexuality or because they use drugs. If you hear a friend saying bad things about minorities or gays or drug users, speak out. People with AIDS suffer twice: because they have the disease, people treat them badly. You can't change the first, but you can change the second. You can fight for the dignity and honor of all people with AIDS.

Make the most of your life by learning how to take care of your mind and body.

Protect Yourself

Drug use can lead to AIDS. If you take drugs with needles, get help to stop. If you can't stop, clean all needles with bleach and rinse with water. Decide when you want to start having sex. When you do have sex, always use a condom. Combining drugs and sex is dangerous. If you do, be extra careful and always use a condom. You are a very important person. Take care of yourself so that you never get HIV.

Help List

In Your Community

Often it is people near your home who know the best places to call. Teachers and counselors have up-to-date information. Your family doctor or church or temple are also good places to start.

Hotlines

You don't have to give your name when you call any of the numbers below. You might be asked where you are or your age, but nothing else.

All numbers beginning with 1-(800) are FREE to the caller. 1-(800) numbers in the United States work only if you call from within the United States. 1-(800) numbers in Canada work only if you call from Canada.

IN THE UNITED STATES

National AIDS Hotline (English)
1-(800)342-AIDS or 1-(800)342-2437
24 hours a day, 7 days a week

National AIDS Hotline SIDA (Spanish)
1-(800)344 SIDA or 344-7432
7 days a week, 8 a.m.–2 p.m.

National AIDS Hotline TTY (Hearing Impaired)
1-(800)AIDS-TTY or 243-7889
Monday-Friday, 10 a.m.-10 p.m.

60 | **Hemophilia Foundation**
1-(212)682-5510
Monday to Friday, 9 a.m.-5 p.m.

National Pediatric HIV Center
1-(800)362-0071
Monday to Friday, 9 a.m.-5 p.m.

National Sexually Transmitted Disease
  Hotline
1-(800)227-8922
Monday to Friday, 8 a.m.-11 p.m.

National Teen AIDS Hotline
1-(800)234-TEEN or 234-8336
Monday to Friday, 5-9 p.m. Eastern Time

IN CANADA

Toronto: AIDS Hotline
1-(416)340-8844 (you may call collect)
Monday to Thursday, 10 a.m.-9 p.m.
Friday, 10 a.m.-5 p.m.

Montreal: AIDS Committee
1-(514)282-9991 (you may call collect)
Monday to Friday, 9 a.m.-10 a.m.

Vancouver: PWA Vancouver
1-(604)893-2250
Monday to Friday, 10 a.m.–5 p.m.
Saturday, 11 a.m.–5 p.m.

Glossary
Explaining New Words

abstinence   Not having or waiting before having sexual intercourse.

AIDS   Acquired immunodeficiency syndrome.

bisexual   Person who has sex with both males and females.

condom   Thin latex covering put over the penis before sex.

drug   Substance taken into the body to change the mood or feelings.

gay   Man who prefers a man as his sexual and life partner, or a woman who prefers a woman as her partner.

hemophilia   Hereditary disease of males that affects blood clotting.

heterosexual   Person who prefers someone of the opposite sex.

HIV   Human immunodeficiency virus.

homosexual   Person who prefers someone of the same sex.

immune system   System of the body that fights infection and disease.

semen   The fluid coming out of a man's penis during sex.

transfusion   Administration of blood or blood products during surgery or to hemophiliacs.

virus   Body cell that takes over another cell.

For Further Reading

Ball, Jacqueline A. *Everything You Need to Know About Drug Abuse*. New York: Rosen Publishing Group, Inc., 1994, rev. ed.

Bell, Ruth. *Changing Bodies, Changing Lives: A Book for Teens on Sex and Relationships*, rev. ed. New York: Random House Vintage Books, 1992.

Draimin, Barbara. *Everything You Need to Know When a Parent Has AIDS*. New York: Rosen Publishing Group, 1993.

Hein, Karen, M.D. *AIDS: Trading Fears for Facts*. New York: Consumers Union, 1989.

Madaras, Lynda. *Lynda Madaras Talks to Teens about AIDS*. New York: Newmarket Press, 1988.

Shire, Amy. *Everything You Need to Know About Being HIV-Positive*. New York: Rosen Publishing Group, Inc., 1994.

Taylor, Barbara. *Everything You Need to Know About AIDS*. New York: Rosen Publishing Group, Inc., 1992 rev. ed.

Index

A

acquired immunodeficiency
    syndrome, *see* AIDS
Africa, AIDS in, 16
AIDS, 7–11
    acquired from drug use,
      19–24
    acquired from sex, 25–31
    defined, 14–18
    preventing, 34–42, 55–58
alcohol, 10, 19, 33, 40–41, 42
Alcoholics Anonymous, 11,
    53
anal intercourse, 31–33
antibodies, 14
anus, 31–33
AZT, 55

B

behavior, altered by drugs,
    23–24, 38
bisexual, 10, 25, 28–29, 42
bleach, cleaning needle with, 22,
    58
blood
    donation, 22
    HIV carried in, 29
    transfusion, 12, 23
body fluids, 29

C

cancer, 16–17
caring, 57
chlamydia, 38
cocaine, 19, 33, 41, 53
condom, 23, 38, 42, 58
    refusal to use, 39–40
counselor, 11, 38, 46, 47,
    49–50

choosing, 52
    individual, 50
crack cocaine, 8–9, 19
cycle, drug use, 47–49

D

detox program, 10–11
discrimination, anti-gay, 28
drug
    addiction, 11, 43–44, 46
    injection, 16, 25, 40, 58

E

education, of peers, 56–57

F

friends, talking to, 50

G

gay, 11, 26–28
gonorrhea, 38

H

heart disease, 16
help, seeking, 46–49
heroin, 12, 21, 53
herpes, 38
heterosexual, 25–26
HIV, 7–11
    defined, 12–13
    and dirty needles, 21–22
    and unprotected sex, 25–31
homophobia, fighting, 57
homosexual, 16–17, 25
human immunodeficiency virus,
    see HIV

I

infant, HIV passed to, 12, 31

64

L
lesbian, 26–28
listening, need for, 17

M
marijuana, 19, 23, 33, 41, 45

N
name-calling, 34
Narcotics Anonymous, 53
needles, drug injection, 11
    cleaning, 19–20, 22, 42,
        58
    dirty, 12, 19
nonoxynol-9, 39

O
oral intercourse, 31

P
peer counselor, 53
penis, 29, 31, 39
pneumonia, 16
prejudice, 17, 28

R
racism, fighting, 57
rectum, 31

S
secret
    language, 19
    sharing, 8
self-esteem, 34

self-help group, 53
semen, 29, 31, 39
sexually transmitted diseases
    (STDs), 9, 36–38
sexual orientation, 25
sexual transmission, 29–31
sex
    bisexual, 29–30
    heterosexual, 26
    homosexual, 26–28
    protected, 26
    unprotected, 16, 23, 25, 28
signs, of drug use, 19–21
sodomy, 31–33
sperm, 29
steroids, 12, 21
suicide, 50–51
support group, 11, 53
syphilis, 9, 38

T
testing, HIV, 9, 14, 38
treatment, addiction, 42–53

U
United States, AIDS in, 16

V
vaginal fluid, 29, 31
vaginal intercourse, 31

W
willpower, lowered, 33, 40

About the Author

Barbara Draimin is a social work administrator for the Division of AIDS Services in New York City. She designs and implements programs for children and their families who have AIDS. The Division serves over 2,500 families with AIDS.

Dr. Draimin received a Doctorate of Social Welfare from the City University of New York and master's degrees from the Hunter College School of Social Work and Boston University School of Education.

She has also written *Coping When a Parent Has AIDS*.

Photo Credits

Cover photo by Maje Waldo; all other phots by Louren Piperno.